Creating a Fine Art Entry Table

A Master Class

Robert Ortiz

Schiffer Publishing Ltd
4880 Lower Valley Road Atglen, Pennsylvania 19310

Schiffer Books are available at special discounts for bulk purchases for sales promotions or premiums. Special editions, including personalized covers, corporate imprints, and excerpts can be created in large quantities for special needs. For more information contact the publisher:

Published by Schiffer Publishing Ltd.
4880 Lower Valley Road
Atglen, PA 19310
Phone: (610) 593-1777; Fax: (610) 593-2002
E-mail: Info@schifferbooks.com

For the largest selection of fine reference books on this and related subjects, please visit our web site at **www.schifferbooks.com**
We are always looking for people to write books on new and related subjects. If you have an idea for a book please contact us at the above address.

This book may be purchased from the publisher.
Include $5.00 for shipping.
Please try your bookstore first.
You may write for a free catalog.

In Europe, Schiffer books are distributed by
Bushwood Books
6 Marksbury Ave.
Kew Gardens
Surrey TW9 4JF England
Phone: 44 (0) 20 8392-8585; Fax: 44 (0) 20 8392-9876
E-mail: info@bushwoodbooks.co.uk
Website: www.bushwoodbooks.co.uk
Free postage in the U.K., Europe; air mail at cost.

Other Schiffer Books on Related Subjects

American Furniture of the 19th Century. Eileen and Richard Dubrow. ISBN: 0764310801. $39.95
American Furniture: Seventeenth, Eighteenth and Nineteenth Century Styles. Helen Comstock. ISBN: 0916838285. $44.95
American Furniture: The Federal Period, 1788-1825. Charles F. Montgomery. ISBN: 0764314068. $75.00
Creating Coffee Tables: An Artistic Approach. Craig Stevens. ISBN: 0764306235. $29.95
Dunbar: Fine Furniture of the 1950s. Preface by Leslie Piña. ISBN: 0764310534. $39.95

Library of Congress Control Number: 2008929572

Covers and book designed by: Bruce Waters
Type set in Goudy Oldstyle/Trajan Pro

ISBN: 978-0-7643-3071-1
Printed in China

Biography

My mother and father, born on the island of Vieques, Puerto Rico, came to New York in 1935 and '37. I grew up in Greenwich Village, where I studied classical piano beginning at age five. At fourteen, I left home and entered a Catholic religious teaching order, leaving that life just before I finished college with a degree in Spanish Literature and education.

In my twenties, I taught high school and later played music on the college coffee house circuit. In 1984, when I was thirty-four, I came across George Nakashima's book, *The Soul of a Tree*. Within three years I had set off on my own with the hope of designing, making, and selling my own line of furniture. Twenty-one years later I'm still at it and fortunate enough to have two lines of furniture named after each of my children, Sofia and Daniel.

Dedication

For Lilly May Highland, my piano teacher. Her hope was simply to teach me to play the piano. Though I did not know it at the time, she introduced me to a world where race and nationality did not matter but where I would be judged and valued by how well I dedicated myself to my craft and my calling. Without her gift, I would never have discovered this road that I travel.

ACKNOWLEDGMENTS

First and foremost, I would like to thank my wife and the photographer of this book, Pamela Cardullo Ortiz, for her willingness to take on this role with this project. Besides being the photographer, she was also the one who kept me focused, encouraged me when I was discouraged, and helped me laugh at myself when I wondered why I ever wanted to write a book in the first place.

Secondly, and just as importantly, I want to thank my children Sofia and Daniel. They are twelve and nine years old respectively. They endured countless hours "in the shop" when photographs were being taken and the table was being made. More than anyone else, they help me keep a perspective on what is really important in my life and they help me to laugh...a lot!

Connie Robinson has worked with me for seven years. She is the Zen-Mistress of sanding. Her understanding of sanding and her skills in this area are beyond exceptional. Without her efforts, this project would never have been finished on time.

Brenda Foehrkolb finishes every piece that goes out the door. Though she is an artist in her own right, I am forever thankful that she is willing to work here when her talents and artist's eye are needed.

I have known Bob Ramsey for twelve years, but only recently did I come to know that he is a wizard at the computer. His efforts in producing the patterns for this book and his willingness to produce them, within my unreasonable time frame, were invaluable.

Nothing that you are reading here would have been possible had Peter Schiffer not come into my shop, unbeknownst to me, one afternoon early in 2007. He returned several months later and then took an even greater risk. He asked me to consider writing a book. I especially thank him for his act of faith in me.

Lastly, thanks to Jeff Snyder, my editor, confessor, voice of encouragement at the other end of the phone, and photography professor all in one.

CONTENTS

INTRODUCTION

I am a self taught woodworker. I never took a shop or woodworking class. By helping my father and uncle, as a boy, I learned how to use hand tools and fix things around the house. By the time I was thirty, I had also learned the fundamentals of plumbing and electricity and carpentry while renovating houses during the summer. At that time, I was a high school Spanish teacher in Washington, D.C. In 1984, I came across George Nakashima's book, *The Soul of a Tree,* and decided that I wanted to learn furniture making. I spent the next year reading, studying, and absorbing as much as I could about making furniture. I purchased several books on making Shaker furniture, including Thomas Moser's book on the subject.

In 1985 I went to work for two cabinet makers in Baltimore. My hands arrived early. By that I mean that I quickly learned the skills that allowed me to make doors that worked. They swung open and closed and they did not fall apart. I could make drawers that opened and closed smoothly and held useful things in a cabinet. We were a small shop. There were seven of us and most of the work that we performed was high-end millwork, residential and commercial cabinetry, and furniture. I learned how to read plans, prepare cut lists, construct case work, and finish wood with oil and lacquer. Most importantly, I learned how to get work "out the door" in a timely fashion. After two years, I set off on my own.

In the beginning, the road was not as smooth or as straight as I thought that it would be for me. For the first eight years of my self-employed, woodworking, business life, I made other people's designs and copied existing styles. I turned down work that did not "speak to me." My family bloodlines run from the factories and garment district of New York City to the sugar cane fields and plantation kitchens of Spanish colonial era Puerto Rico. If my ancestors had a style of furniture in their home, it tended to be that which had been cast off by others or those things that could be built from "recycled" materials. For this reason I think that traditional furniture or what is also referred to as "period furniture" has never had a great appealed to me. My people, my family, and I were never – and continue not to be – a part of that period or tradition. I think that I can appreciate period furniture for what it is, but I am not naturally drawn to it.

Having said that, I do have to admit that I was also very fortunate to share my first woodworking shop with furniture maker and conservator, Walter Raynes, of Baltimore, Maryland. His conservation work for some of the pre-eminent collectors of eighteenth and nineteenth century American furniture allowed me to see, close at hand, some of the best furniture ever made – anywhere. The works of many of these long gone masters challenged what I had read and continue to read in woodworking books and magazines and freed me from the tyranny of the "right way" to do things. I got to see, close at hand, the importance of proportion, line, shadow, and grain selection. Those old timers knew that when we view a painting, sculpture or piece of furniture, we take it in as a first impression and then we begin to absorb it as we run our eyes over it to inspect the details. In hindsight, I served my apprenticeship in my shop and at my machines, learning about proportion, line, and shadow, discovering how line plays with, and affects, different wood grains. In short, my work was providing me with the knowledge base that formal training or education normally imparts.

My eyes took longer to arrive. For eight years I made other people's designs, sometimes copying a style, but most often working from a set of drawings that were given to me. Finally, in 1996, a client asked me to design a coffee table for her living room. I decided that it was time for me to find my own "voice" and attempted to find what was common to the two major influences that I could identify in my furniture leanings, i.e. Shaker – all those books that I was drawn to, and Japanese – Mr. Nakashima's book. From this one coffee table the *Sofia Line* was born. Of the thirty-some pieces that are presently in the *Sofia Line* collection, the entry table is my favorite piece.

To my mind, the making of a piece of furniture is not unlike the cooking of a good meal. In order for a special meal to be served, it has to be planned. The cook will be sure that he or she has the equipment needed to prepare the feast. The chef will want to decide which side dishes will best complement the main dish, which ingredients will set off the right combination of flavors, and the proper sequence of preparation that will result in the different courses being served so that hot things stay hot and cool things arrive chilled. Once these details are decided upon, only then does the cook begin to purchase the food. There are different cuts of meat, different grades, and various portion sizes to consider. Choosing fresh and good quality ingredients will ensure that the meal is a success, not just in terms of taste, but also visually, in the manner of its presentation.

A well made piece of furniture is not unlike the meal that we just talked about. It needs to be planned and I do not just mean in terms of height, depth, and width, but also in terms of how it will be viewed. Will it be seen from a distance, up close or both? What are our ingredients going to be? What type of wood and what grain patterns? What is the function of the piece? Also, just as you cannot cook a low grade cut of beef and expect it to taste like filet mignon; you can not purchase a common grade of wood and expect it to turn out like that gorgeous piece that you saw in a magazine, at a show, or in a book.

One final and very important thought before we set out on our journey. There is probably no mistake that you will make that I have not made several times over. This is something that I always remind my apprentices and anyone who asks for advice. Most beginning woodworkers get to work thinking that they should try, as much as possible, to avoid making mistakes, and tend to get upset with themselves when they do. If this aptly describes you, then I have a question for you...do you think that Michael Jordan would tell himself before a game, "I can't miss any shots?" What about the great chef Emeril Lagasse? Was it ever his goal not to burn anything? Of course not! If you are in the kitchen, you will burn things. Even if you are an MVP, Hall of Fame, basketball player, you will miss shots. To have that expectation is, I think, to misunderstand the task at hand. If you are making things with your hands and using your head, you will make mistakes. I think you have the wrong expectation or are asking the wrong question. A better goal, one that is more realistic and that will help you build confidence and skill is this, *be purposeful in everything that you do.* In short, pay attention! It all matters. When he walked onto the basketball court, Michael Jordan did nothing that was sloppy, casual or indifferent. Chef Emeril is focused, precise, and aware of his court, the kitchen. I have no doubt that his knives are sharp and of very good quality, and that his kitchen has good lighting. Oprah on her TV show, Tiger Woods on the golf course...they all know that it's the little things, the preparation, and focus of the task at hand that allows them to succeed. And if you are prepared when something goes awry, as it almost always does, the strategy for a recovery is usually available. You are no different than these great achievers. You can do what they have learned to do. Be purposeful in what you do in your shop. It all matters. For the musician, the instrument is his or her tool. For you, the woodworker, your tools are your instruments, just as the golf clubs are for Tiger, the knives are for Emeril, and the ball is for Michael. Your arena is your workshop, even if it is only a humble table in the corner of your basement. But if you focus and pay attention when you are there, if you are purposeful while you are there, I believe that you can make beautiful furniture that will reward you for a lifetime. Let's get started.

A word about measurements...I purchase all of my materials from the mill "in the rough." This allows me to be sure that I can prepare all of my parts to be flat and square. The *Sofia Entry Table* base requires legs that are 1 1/2" thick, so I purchase 8/4 or 2 inch thick material. The upper and lower stretchers are 1" thick, so I purchase 5/4 or 1 1/4 inch thick material. Some woodworkers will purchase material that is already "dressed" or S2S (surfaced two sides) to its final thickness. If you purchase your material in this manner, make sure that it is flat and has no twists. I will use both measurements in this book to help avoid confusion. The actual measurement of a board will also be given. So a 1" (4/4) thick by 5" wide by 15 1/2" long board will be that very measurement.

Many homes have in their entry way a piece of furniture that serves several purposes. On one level, this is a piece that greets everyone who walks through the door. In some settings, its job is to give a first impression of the home. In other homes, it will catch whatever the person entering may have in their hands, the newspaper, the day's mail, a set of keys, scarf and gloves in the wintertime, or perhaps a hat. In some settings it may hold a piece of pottery or a family photo. For a special occasion, fresh flowers may be placed on it to greet arriving guests.

Since this is a piece that may be seen from both a distance and up close, I want the Sofia Entry Table to give two impressions, a quick one from far away and a more subtle and detailed one from up close. From far away I want the viewer to have a sense of the table's form, a quick impression, one of movement. If I had a sketchpad, I could draw that with four or five line strokes in five seconds like this.

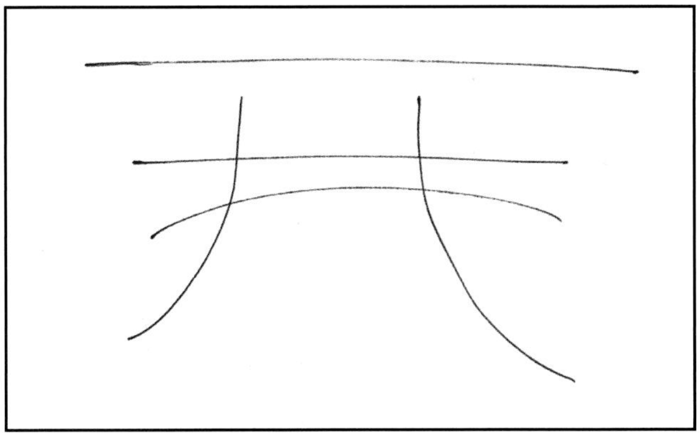

I don't want a bold wood grain to interfere with this first impression. The truth is that other things will distract our entering visitor, saying hello to the host or taking off a coat, so visually, the table has to do its job quickly.

Sofia Entry Table in Cherry and Wenge. *Courtesy of Barry and Susan Koh,* painting, *Harbor,* by Valerie Smith, Dracaena Drago Vase by Michael and Christina Adcock.

Detail, Sofia Entry Table in Walnut and Cherry. *Courtesy Betty and Chris Conyers.*

Perhaps later, when our visitor is less rushed and taking in his or her surroundings and is standing closer to the entry table, its other qualities will begin to emerge. Here, up close, one can now take in the previously unseen details: a seemingly floating top, a beautiful one piece slab top with a natural edge asking to be touched, exposed joinery that is highlighted by shadow and surprising grain texture.

Detail, Sofia Entry Table, *Courtesy Barry and Susan Koh.*

Detail, Sofia Entry Table, *Courtesy Betty and Chris Conyers.*

Using Grain to Enhance Your Design

When I'm making a piece of furniture, I imagine myself painting a picture. The difference is that it's not two-dimensional and it's not on canvas, it's on wood. The painter/artist uses brush strokes – subtle, bold, bright, dark, thick, etc. For me, I choose my brush strokes by choosing woods of different grains, figure, texture, and color. I have a plan, even if it's only a mental one of what type of grain I will put where. It's like cooking. If you serve a meal where everything is spicy hot or all the tastes are strong, the meal will lack subtlety of taste, variety or surprise. Furniture where all the components are figured or the grain pattern conflicts with the lines of the piece has little appeal for me. If you are making furniture you should be talking to yourself…a lot. (Just keep your voice down so that no one wonders what you're really doing down in your shop!) Do not make a leg out of any old piece of wood because it happens to be slightly bigger than what you need. Ask yourself if it has the grain pattern that you want in a particular place. Does it relate to the grain in the other legs? Does it work with or against the lines of your project? If you can incorporate this conversation with yourself as you build your furniture, I believe that you will raise your efforts to a new level.

I like cook books with photographs of beautifully presented and great looking food that makes me say, "I want a taste of that!" So I thought it would be fun to make the table for this book with the same idea of using exquisitely figured and colored woods. My hope is to make a piece that will be visually inspiring. I have chosen to make the top from a 16" wide plank of rare curly bubinga. The shelf slats will also be made of bubinga with a quieter quarter sawn straight grain. The vertical surfaces will be made of wenge, an exotic wood with a semi-sweet chocolate color that will contrast nicely with the bubinga. Wenge is not an easy wood to work with. It tears out easily when cross cutting, so sharp cutters are essential and accurate scoring is a must before cutting on the table saw. On the plus side, it polishes up nicely when finely sanded and takes an oil finish beautifully.

These are not woods for the novice. I usually make this table using cherry and walnut or cherry for the top and shelf and wenge for the base. I recommend that you make your table with woods that you have worked with in the past.

The Sofia Entry Table base, aside from the shelf, is made up of nine pieces of wood: four legs, two lower stretchers that hold the fourteen shelf slats, two short upper stretchers, and a top stretcher. Here is my mental picture of how I want the base to look. The front legs will have a straight grain to enhance the curve of the leg. The back legs will have a slightly bolder grain, a nice surprise that won't be evident on first seeing the table but which will be discovered later on. The lower arched stretcher, which holds the shelf slats, will have straight grain to complement the quarter sawn grain of the shelf pieces and to frame the arch. The two short stretchers, going from the front to the back leg, are pretty much hidden in shadow under the top and behind the leg. I don't usually concern myself very much with the grain here. You may decide that you would choose to highlight different things by choosing woods of different grains than I have. That is just fine. Whatever choices of wood and grain selection you make, just be purposeful about them, think them through.

Lights! Camera! Action! Everyone knows those words from Hollywood movies. It's no accident that before anything can happen, the lights have to be up; they have to be focused on the action and the scene has to be well lit. Your shop is no different than the movie set. Before you can act, make a cut, layout for a joint or turn on a machine, you should be set up for success. If you can't see what you're working on clearly, you are short changing yourself, not to mention straining your eyes.

Most of the joinery in the *Sofia Entry Table* is exposed with "no place to hide" as I like to say. I cut all of the joinery on the table saw. To ensure that I can see my knife marks easily and clearly, I bring a spotlight to my table saw. I don't simply rely on the overhead shop lighting. The spotlight will accentuate the knife cut on the wood. The spotlight helps me focus my attention on the precise place that I am working and thus keeps me from getting tired as the day progresses. If you try this, I am sure that the quality of your work and joinery will improve and you'll make better furniture. I use a simple clip on light that I purchased at the local hardware store for $6.00. I put a halogen spotlight in it and duct taped it to a cheap tripod stand. With every passing year I use it even more! Unfortunately, when we were photographing for this book we had to eliminate the light, but try it and I am sure that the quality of your work will improve.

Okay, now. Lights! Camera! Table saw!

Producing the "Bill of Fare"

For me, the "Bill of Fare" is the name that I give to the actual pieces that will become the parts that I need to make my furniture. So now that I've gone through the process of deciding how I choose my material, it's time to mill the wood. I usually cut my lengths two inches longer than I actually need just in case a chip flies off the end during milling. So if I need a 32" long leg, I'll rough cut at 34". A 15 1/2" board will be cut at 17 1/2" and so on. Here is my "rough bill of fare," i.e. the wood before I joint and plane it so that it is square and flat. All of these pieces are made of wenge on this project.

1. 4 legs from 2 planks 36 inches long by 5 1/2" wide by 2" (8/4) thick
2. 2 lower stretchers 49 inches long by 4 1/2" wide by 1 1/4" (5/4) thick
3. 2 front to back stretchers 17 inches long by 5 1/2" wide by 1" (4/4) thick
4. 1 upper stretcher 49 inches long by 2 1/2" wide by 1 1/4" (5/4) thick
5. 1 or 2 leg, test pieces 2" (8/4) by 1 3/4" and about 12" long
6. 1 or 2 front to back stretcher test pieces 5 1/2" by 1" (4/4) about 12" long

At this point I joint, plane, and sand all the pieces, even the test pieces down to 1 1/2 inches for the legs and 1 inch for everything else. I use my wide belt sander to insure uniform thicknesses. I realize that you may not have this equipment but you can still do this by hand. I used to "in the old days." You may also be able to call a local cabinet shop and have them sand your pieces at their shop rate. If they are willing to do this for you, ask what they will charge, and besides paying them their hourly rate, bring along some baked goods, a bottle of wine or a six pack of beer and most likely they will gladly provide you with this service in the future.

If you are going to hand sand, plane or scrape the pieces, rough mill as close as you can and then get everything to the correct thickness. I sand everything to120 grit at this point. This may seem like an unusual time in the process to sand but over the years I have found that if I have parts to a uniform thickness, my joinery, especially exposed joinery will fit together cleaner and more precisely.

I am now ready to cut my parts to length. I rely on all of my cuts being square when they leave the table saw. Whatever you use, a miter gauge, cross cut sled, chop saw or hand held saw, make sure your cuts are square. I want to be able to clamp my parts together later on and know that they will pull together squarely. If the cuts are off, so will the table or anything else that you make for that matter. I use a cross cut sled, but I also place a sacrificial 1/4" piece of plywood behind the pieces that I'm cutting in order to minimize any tear out. I will also have a piece of sandpaper on a block and as I finish cross cutting my legs, I will slightly bevel the end grain to help prevent accidental chipping as I am handling the pieces. This may seem like a waste of time but I assure you, chip out one piece and you'll spend much more time repairing each knick or chip.

Here is the "Actual Bill of Fare," that is, the exact dimensions of the parts that will make up the base. They are:

1. 4 legs from two planks, 35" long by 5 1/2" wide by 1 1/2" thick
2. 2 lower stretchers 47" long by 4 1/2" wide by 1" thick
3. 2 front to back stretchers 15" long by 5" wide by 1" thick
4. 1 upper stretcher 46" long by 2" wide by 1" thick
5. 1 or 2 leg test pieces 1 1/2" square by about 10" long
6. 1 or 2 front to back test pieces 5" wide, by the same thickness as the stretchers above by about 12" long

TEST LEG MORTISE

PRECISE MARKING IS THE KEY TO PRECISE CUTTING.

When I lay out curved patterns to cut on any parts, I use a number 2 pencil. The thickness of the lead is easy to see. I make the curved cut on the band saw. If I make my cut just barely touching the line, I can clean it up without too much work. This is, however, the only time that I use such a broad instrument for marking.

When it comes to laying out joints I will only use a razor knife for the rest of my marking. You don't need to purchase an expensive or special tool. A small, plastic razor knife, available at the check out counter of any hardware store will do just fine. If the tip gets dulled or no longer makes a clean cut, break it off to expose a clean edge. Sometimes low tech can be just as good, or better, than expensive and fancy.

When I am making the cuts at the table saw, I will take a work lamp and shine light directly on the cut so that I can see precisely where the razor mark is. If you are determined to use a pencil, I would recommend that you use a mechanical pencil no thicker than .05 millimeters, or learn how to shave a lead pencil to a razor point. I truly believe that nothing will raise the level of your woodworking skill more than being disciplined about marking purposefully.

Making the Legs

Now the real work of making the *Sofia Entry Table* begins. The next step is not unlike sewing. We need to draw the pattern of the leg curve onto the four legs so that we can cut them out. You will need to make a pattern that is 3 1/4" wide by 32 1/8" long referring to the scale pattern that I have provided. In all the scale drawings that I have provided, each box is an actual 1" square.

You can use construction paper or a heavier weight paper that you can purchase at an art supply or stationery store to make your pattern. I use heavy paper, because I can experiment with different curves and simply cut another one if I don't like what I see. Using a razor knife, cut the curve side first and leave the straight side wide. Once you are happy with the curve, cut the straight line at the back so that the leg is 1 1/2" at the top and 3 1/4" at the bottom.

Lay your pattern on the 35" by 5 1/2" board and, using a #2 pencil, trace the leg neatly and carefully, in one motion, if possible. Avoid overlapping lines that could confuse you when you are at the band saw. I have lost count of the number of times that I traced my lines without being careful and found myself, cutting at the band saw, trying to figure out which line I was supposed to be following…in the middle of a cut!

Since we are cutting 2 legs out of one plank, lay them out so that the straight part of the leg is to the outside of the board with the wider part of the leg at opposite ends of the board.

FRONT LEG

BACK LEG

ENTRY TABLE PATTERN
BACK LEG
BACK LEG
FRONT LEG
FRONT LEG

Separate the two legs at the band saw. Where the two legs come close, I usually split the difference. Once you have done that to the four legs, take them to the table saw and cut them down to their actual length using your template as the guide. The length should be 32 1/8".

You are only going to cut the outside curved line of the leg. In order to easily cut the open mortise at the top of the leg, and the lap joint for the lower stretcher later on, we still need the back of the leg to be straight as a reference point on the miter gauge.

Now that the four legs are marked, I take them to the band saw and before I begin to cut, I make sure that the band saw table is at 90 degrees to the blade. Simply hold the leg on the outside of the blade and be sure that it makes contact over the entire length. The blade that I usually use here is a 1/4" steel blade with 4 teeth per inch. Take your time making the cut and you will spend less time cleaning up the cut. Notice that there was a problem area in one of the boards that I used. However, having examined the board, I am confident that this will not affect the leg structurally or visually.

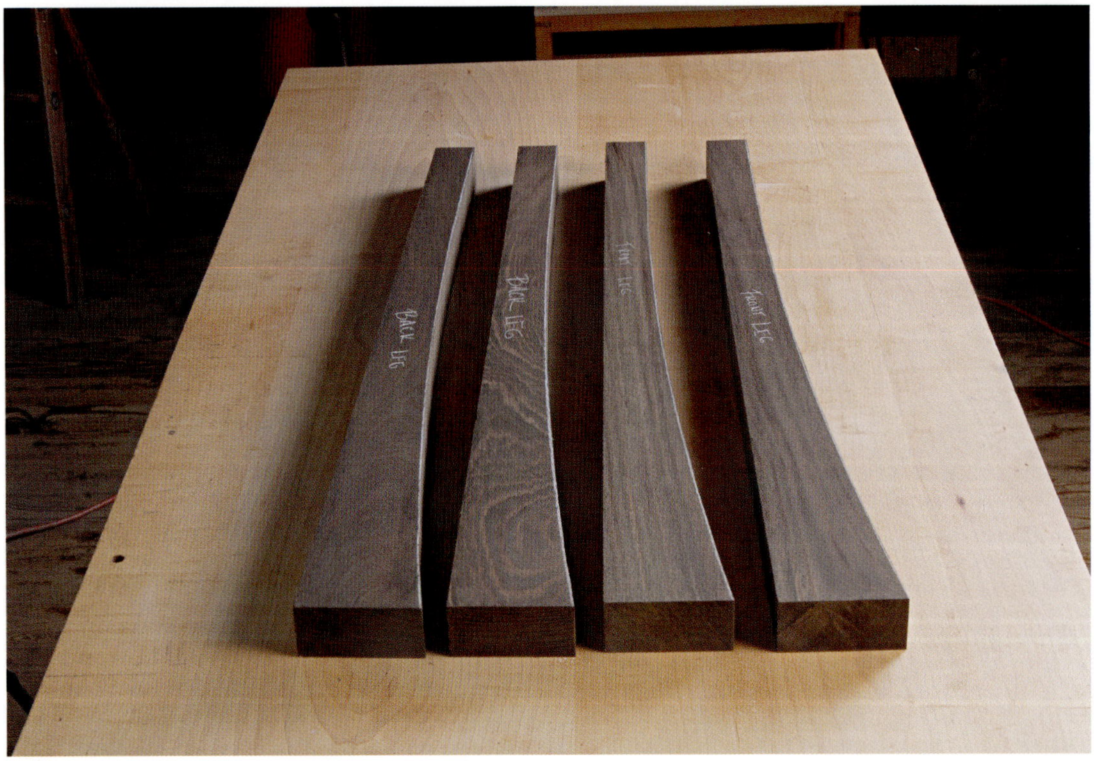
BACK LEG
BACK LEG
FRONT LEG

Once the four cuts are made, the band saw cut needs to be made smooth. You can do this on an oscillating spindle sander, with a spoke shave or simply with a palm sander, making sure that you stay square.

I use the shaper to do this since I make many of these parts. I have a jig that I have designed, which allows me to vary the width and length of the leg. I use this jig to make about 15 different variations on the *Sofia Line* leg. The width at the top of the legs for the entry table should now be 1 1/2" by 1 1/2".

There was a small amount of tear out in the problem area mentioned on page 23. I will add a small amount of 5-minute clear epoxy. Use only clear epoxy. You can purchase this at any hardware store. Follow the directions. Mix just a small amount. I used less than you would use on a toothbrush to clean your teeth. Let it stand for a few hours – even if it says 5 minutes. If you try to cut or sand it before it fully cures, it will turn gummy. We will examine the repair that we made at the end of construction.

I will sand the curved part of the leg using 120 grit (120 microns) sandpaper. Clamping a pair of legs together helps with assuring that the legs are uniform and remain square. When I have finished sanding all four legs, I will stand them up and identify each one. I use the designations (fl) front left, (fr) front right, (bl) back left, and (br) back right. It will be imperative that you clearly mark parts as you go along.

FL
BL
FRONT LEG
BACK LEG

BACK LEG

BR
FR
FL
BL
FRONT LEG
BACK LEG

Cutting the Open Mortise

There are obviously many different ways of cutting an open mortise. I make my mortises at the table saw. This comes from my days of working in that first cabinet shop where accuracy and speed were the key. I use a tenoning jig to make the mortises. That's right, a tenoning jig to make mortises. As I mentioned at the start of this book, I'm self-taught. I don't necessarily use all tools as the manufacturer intended. Just because the maker doesn't think of using the tool differently doesn't mean that I can't or you can't. But it does mean that if you are going to bend or break a rule, you had better think it through in terms of safety, reliability, and accuracy.

You could use a mortising attachment on a drill press. Drill presses, however, tend to tear out on the back side of a cut, so you will want to set up the cut so that you can avoid this problem.

You also need to pay attention to the saw blade that you use. My saw blade of choice is a Forrest Woodworker II. It's an expensive blade, but it cuts flawlessly with no tear out, and when you have exposed joinery, as we have in this project, you can't afford any. Whatever you choose, make sure it's sharp and clean.

The open mortise on the four legs will be 2" high by 3/8" wide. This will leave 9/16 of an inch to the left and right of the mortise at the top of the leg.

At this point I'd recommend that you straighten out your table saw area. Put away all tools except for your square, miter gauge, and razor knife. Get out your shop light and place it so that it will shine on your table saw top. Place your four legs and two test pieces where you can see them. Raise your saw blade 2" high, set the rip fence to 9/16 of an inch, and set your test piece in the tenoning jig, making side to side adjustments in the jig so that the test piece is touching the fence.

Now move the fence away and carefully make the cut. Remember that our test piece is square and about 10 inches long. After you make the first cut, take the test piece out of the jig. Check to see that your cut is at 9/16".

Lay the leg down and mark with your razor knife the top most point at which the saw blade emerged from the back of the test piece. Now make that cut across the grain. You can then transfer the exact distance of that cut to a marking gauge. I prefer using a combination square. I place my razor blade in the mark and slide the square to the 2" mark and lock it in place. Now rotate the test piece half a turn (180°). Score the opposite side at 2 inches.

Set your test piece back in the jig. The scoring mark that you made at 2 inches should be in the back (you are trying to eliminate tear out). Your first cut will now be parallel to the cut that you are about to make. Reset your fence to 9/16 of an inch. The test piece should now be touching the fence. Lock the test piece in place, move the fence away, and make your cut. You should have about 1/8 of an inch between the two cuts.

Check to see if you got any tear out on the back side. If you did, make any necessary adjustment to your marking gauge to eliminate this. Make another test cut on your other test piece, or flip this piece end to end and try again until you are confident that you have it right. Measure the two cuts that you have. If each is equidistant from the sides and has 1/8 of an inch between the cuts, you are ready to cut the legs.

Take a moment and mark the direction of the cut through the legs; if you don't you will likely make the same mistake that I made early on in making this line of furniture. You'll mistakenly cut the open mortises in the wrong direction, i.e. side to side instead of front to back. I usually use chalk to mark the direction of the cut. Chalk won't mar the wood and comes off easily. Lay all four pieces down in the same direction and score the back side at 2 inches to insure that you will not get tear out. If you use a combination square you can mark the 3/8 width of your mark in pencil on the steel rule and make a more precise score.

Pick up you correct test piece, place it in the jig, and adjust the tenoning jig so that the blade slides easily through the left cut. You won't need to use the fence now.

Once you have it set correctly, switch out the test piece and carefully place your first leg in the jig. Make sure it sits flat on the table with no dust underneath. The leg should sit at 1 1/2" front to back and left to right it should be 1 1/2" at the bottom and 3 1/4" at the top. The curved part should be on the right and the flat side on the left against the flat side of the jig. Lastly, the scored part should be at the back of the leg to prevent tear out. Once you are confident that you've got it, make your cut. Turn off the saw, remove the leg from the jig, and place the next leg in the jig. Repeat this process until you have one cut in each of the four legs.

Next pick up your test piece again, place it in the jig, and adjust the jig so that you can make the second cut. Follow the steps above and repeat it four times. Remember to work methodically; you don't need to rush. Let the saw blade do the work smoothly, cutting its way through the wood. If you push the wood too fast through the saw blade, you may cause the blade to vibrate and will get a sloppy cut. If you cut too slowly, you will get burning as the blade will heat up excessively. Just like in basketball, with a jump shot from the top of the key, you need the "right touch." It's the same when you cut the joinery.

LEG

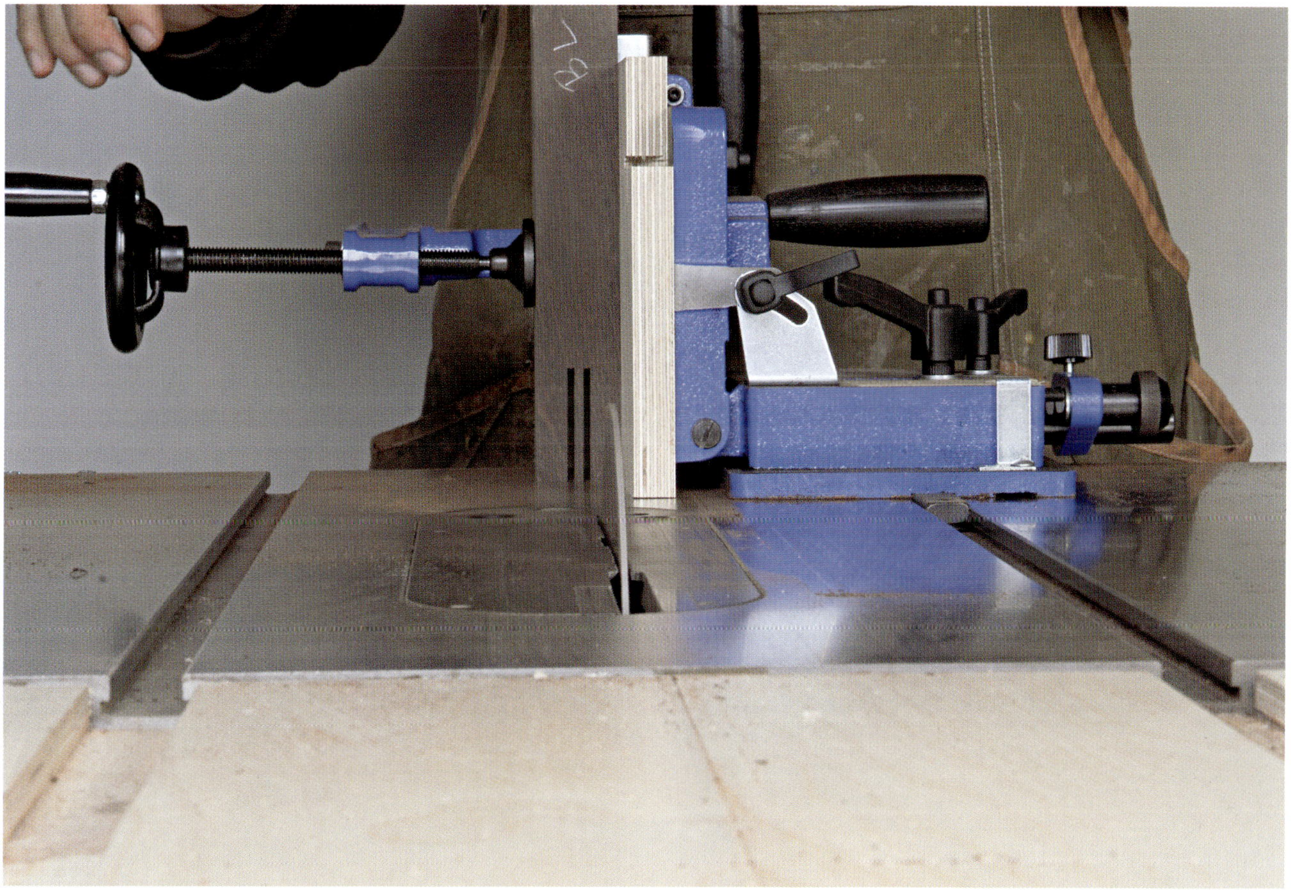

Finally, pick up the test piece one last time, place it in the jig, and move it so that you can clean out the remaining 1/8 inch. Do this on your test piece also if you don't have a lot of experience cleaning out mortise bottoms. You'll be able to practice before going to an actual leg. Make your last cut on all four legs. Don't be alarmed if you find that you were a bit off and the last cut took a hair more than one cut to finish off which means that it's a bit wider than 1/8". As long as your through mortise is centered, you'll be fine.

At this point I stand the legs back up again to help me envision the table. Each of the legs should still be marked, front left, etc. Because I use an alternate tooth bevel blade I will not have a flat bottom, so now I simply take a chisel and create a flat bottom. I score the front of the front legs and the back of the back legs. (Hint: you will actually find that two of the legs are already scored.) I then lay the leg down and take a 3/8 inch chisel and, working back from the score line, make sure that I have a flat bottom. There you have it. This step is done. For what it's worth, I think you've completed the hardest part.

Cutting the Through Tenons on the Front to Back Stretchers

The front to back stretchers are really less complicated than they look. If we break this down, one step at a time, we'll get the stretcher to do three things: 1. provide a decorative element as the stretcher pierces the front and rear legs; 2. join the front and back legs; and 3. provide a staging platform to lift the top above the legs and give the top the appearance of floating.

I don't use a tenoning jig to cut my tenons. I prefer to use a dado blade on the table saw. I use a 1/2 inch wide dado for this cut. Again, my saw blade of choice is a Forrest Manufacturing Co. carbide tipped 8 inch dado set.

We will work with the two front to back stretchers that are 5" wide by 15" long by 1" thick, and also with the one or two test pieces that should be about 10" long. The length of the tenon will be 1 3/4", i.e. the thickness of the leg 1 1/2" plus 1/4" of exposure beyond the leg. The height of the dado blade will be somewhere in the neighborhood of 5/16 on an inch. I stack my dado blade so that it is 1/2" wide. I will then set my fence at 1 1/4", which will allow me to cut a 1 3/4" dado, i.e. the distance to the fence (1 1/4" plus the 1/2" wide cutter.) It is imperative that your test pieces and actual stretchers be cut squarely if you want accurate results. Take the time to set yourself up for success. Make sure that the square you have ***is*** square. Make sure that your miter gauge ***is*** set to cut squarely.

I use my test piece to make test cuts until I am happy with the results. The depth of the tenon is 1 3/4", the shoulders of the tenon are parallel to each other on both faces, and my test piece fits just a bit tight into the mortise.

Fitting Tenons to Mortises

I'm always trying to improve how I make these joints. Here is my preferred method these days. After I make my through tenons, I re-measure the thickness of each one. I can hear some of you at this very moment saying, "They should all be the same!" To which I will respond, "The key word here is *should*, and I don't live in a perfect world and suspect that you don't either." Remember back to Michael Jordan missing baskets and Emeril's cooking going up in flames in the kitchen. What do they do? They adjust. So do I, and if your through mortises are slightly different, you should have a plan to adjust. Here is mine.

I take my dial calipers and measure my tenons. Hopefully they are all pretty close, at least within 1/64th or closer. I will then set my dado blade to cut the tenon so that it will fit in the fattest mortise. What I don't want is a sloppy fit. Remember, this is a visible through tenon. There is no place to hide! I cut all four tenons and then I will individually fine-tune the individual tenon to the corresponding mortise.

This may sound like a lot of work but several years ago I purchased a shoulder plane. Mine is a medium shoulder plane made by Lee Valley Tools. In about thirty seconds, I can fit the tenon perfectly to the mortise. The tool pays for itself every time I use it and the fit is a thing of beauty to behold. If you don't have a shoulder plane you'll want to make your adjustment as I used to with a flat sanding block (to ensure that your mortise stays flat) and coarse sandpaper or perhaps some of you will use a chisel or a fine wood rasp.

Now that your dado blade is set and your fence is where it needs to be, take a moment and label the two actual stretchers. Identify left and right, front and back and even top and bottom. Look at the grain. Which side do you want to see? Or perhaps there is a small flaw that you will want to hide on the inside. Now slowly and carefully begin to cut your tenons. I'd recommend attaching a sacrificial fence to the mitre gauge to eliminate tear out on the stretcher as the dado blade finishes the cross cut.

NOTE WELL: Dado blades leave score marks. In this case, because we are using a half inch dado blade, the deep score marks will be 1/2" apart. The exposed tenon protrudes 1/4" past the tenon. Make sure that you cut the part that will be exposed first so that there is no visible score mark. It's easiest to cut the end first. Just line it up with the cut on the sacrificial fence.

Since the two front to back stretchers that we are now dadoing are wide boards, make sure that they remain flat as you are cutting the tenon on the table saw. When you finish the cuts, your front to back stretchers will be 15" long by 5" wide by 1" thick. At each end there will be a 3/8" tenon that is 1 3/4" long by 5". We now need to cut the tenons down so that they fit the mortises. Only after they are cut down will we individually fit them to their corresponding mortises.

TOP
OUTSIDE
TOP
OUTSIDE
F to BK

Tenon cut away
3/4" x 2 1/2"

I have provided you with a pattern of the "tenon cut away." Make a pattern of it out of heavy cardboard or card stock. Trace the pattern at the top of each stretcher. Mark it clearly on the top of the four tenons as shown.

TOP
OUT SIDE

You will need to cut 2 1/4" off the bottom tenon. The finished tenon needs to be 2" tall (the depth of the mortise) ***plus*** an additional 3/4" (the cut away which raises the top above the legs.) Lay the two boards down so that you can correctly identify which will be the bottom of the board.

Change back to your saw blade. Raise the blade slightly *less* than 1 3/4" (the length of the tenon). Place a tall (4 or 5 inches) auxiliary fence on your mitre gauge that extends about 1 1/2 inches past the saw cut. Move your fence to a shade more than 2 3/4". Standing your test stretcher on end, with the top touching the fence and make your cut. Mark an X on the piece that will be below the tenon. This is the piece that you are going to cut off. Make sure you mark it. I can't tell you how many times I said to myself, "I don't need to mark it, I know how to do this." Then, I get distracted momentarily, and, lo and behold, I've chopped off the wrong end! Do yourself a favor; mark what you're cutting off. Once you're set up correctly and have made the cut successfully on your test piece, pick up your actual front to back stretcher and make the cut. Once you've made the cut, flip the board and cut the tenon at the other end of the board. Repeat this process on the other stretcher.

Now you can chop off the 2 1/8" by 1 3/4" portion. I prefer to do this on my band saw, cutting about 1/16" away from the shoulder of the stretcher. You can also do this with a handsaw or any other way that works for you. I will come back with my chisel and clean the shoulder so that I can get a clean fit when I join the stretcher to the leg. You should now have a 2 3/4" by 1 3/4" long tenon.

While you are at the band saw, cut well **above** the curved line that you drew for the tenon cut-away. I usually cut a fat 1/16" above the line. We will work our way down to the line after we have glued the legs to the stretchers and can create a clean, graceful transition.

Now is the time to fit your tenons to your mortises. I use my shoulder plane to get the precise fit that I want on each leg. Remember, each mortise should correspond to a leg that we previously marked (fr, fl, br, bl). Do not glue yet. That comes later.

You can arch the lower portion of the front to back stretchers at this point. I prefer a deep arch, about 1 inch, but you might prefer something less deep. Put your design skills to work here and decide what you would like this to look like. I have used the radii of paint buckets, drywall buckets, dishes—you name it—to make my curves. Experiment with different shapes.

FL
BL
BR
FR
FRONT LEG
BACK LEG

Find the center point, mark it, and make an arch or segment of a circle at the bottom on both left and right front to back stretchers. Cut out the arch on your band saw and clean up your saw marks using a spoke shave, sand paper, or drum sander.

F to B
TOP
OUTSIDE
FL
BL

OUT SIDE

MAKING A KERF TO ATTACH THE BASE TO THE TOP

There are many different ways of attaching the top of a piece to its base. I am not averse to using mechanical fasteners where appropriate. Sometimes I will make my own. In the case of the entry table, I use a metal table clip, which I will paint black to better conceal it in the shadows beneath the top. They are made by McFeeley's Square Drive Tools. The clip will allow the plank to move independently of the base during seasonal movement and still secure the base firmly to the top.

Dry fit the front to back aprons with their corresponding legs, left side on left, right side on right and front and back in their correct places. Now with a piece of chalk mark the upper **inside** of the left and right stretchers. We are going to run a 1/4" deep, 1/8" wide saw kerf, 3/8" down from the top edge on the inside of the stretcher. We will use a metal clip that we will paint black to secure the top to the base in this manner.

Take the stretchers that you marked with chalk, set your fence at 3/8" and raise the blade 1/4" high. Take any flat piece of wood or plywood that you have lying around and make a test piece. NOTE WELL: Do not raise the blade higher than 1/4" or you will cut into the tenon cut away (the detail that makes the table top appear to float.) Cut the slot into each inside top part of the stretcher as shown in the photo.

Making the Lower Arched Stretchers

I have provided you with a scaled half pattern for the lower arched stretchers. Remember that the scale is each square represents 1 square inch. I used to make my curves by using heavy stock paper and then transferring that to 1/4" plywood. I now use a drawing bow, made by Lee Valley Tools, for most of my curved surfaces. The curves are true (no flat spots) and, in a matter of seconds, I can get an infinite number of curves. I don't even need to use paper; I go right to the wood. Here's how I do it.

I start by taking my two 47" by 4 1/2" boards and find the mid-point of each. I mark the mid-point on the wood. Then I determine the width of the board at the mid-point. Next I take my drawing bow and adjust it until the center point of the bow, while touching the point of the height at the middle, also touches the two bottom ends of the board. Once I get this established, I draw my line. You can start by drawing a line at 23 1/2" i.e. at the mid-point of our 47" stretcher. Use the pattern to draw half the arch, flip the paper and draw the other half.

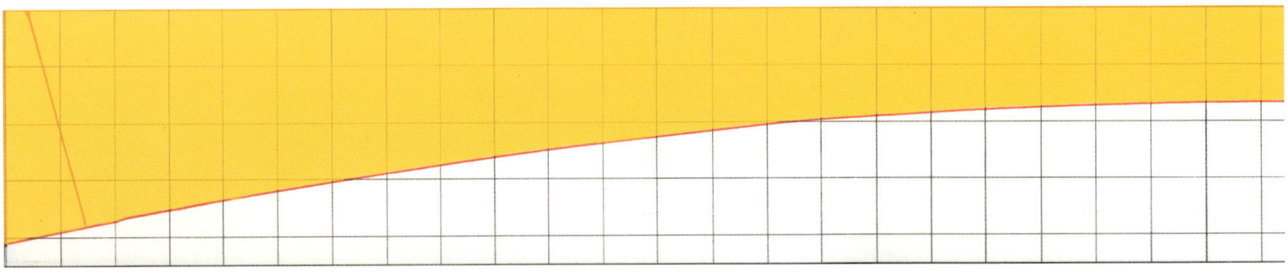

23 3/4
MID POINT

1 1/16

Then I go to the band saw and cut the arch approximately 1/16" proud (wide) of my line. After I have band sawn both pieces, I take both pieces back to my bench.

I then work my way down to the line using a spoke shave. This step usually goes pretty quickly and you have the satisfaction of using a hand tool – no dust, no noise, just nice shavings on the shop floor. If you're not comfortable with a spoke shave, you could use spindle sander or even a random orbital sander.

Regardless of what you use, make sure that your curves are "fair," i.e. true and graceful, no flat spots, bumps or dips. Take the time to sight down the length of the curve. It's easier to see slight imperfections to your curve that way. The arch should measure about 1 1/2" in the center.

Now that the arched lower stretchers are cut, I would recommend that you sand them – front, back, top, and bottom – to their final grit. In the shop here we sand to 400. I think that you should at least sand to 240 grit. You want to do this now because you are going to cut an open half lap joint 1/4 deep into the front and back legs. If you cut the joint now and sand the arch later, you will get a sloppy fit. If you sand now, and then make your marks to cut the half lap joint, the fit will be tighter.

DEWALT

Joining the Lower Arched Stretchers to the Legs

In order to cut an open half lap joint into the legs, I prefer to stand the unfinished table base up. I dry fit the right front and back legs to the front to back stretcher and do the same with the left legs. Since the mortise and tenon has been fine-tuned to fit together it should be fairly easy to assemble these. By putting these parts together I can help myself visualize how the table will look. I can see how the grain of the legs interact with the grain of the stretchers, etc.

I start by going to my work bench and drawing parallel lines 15" long and 36" apart from each other. That's right, I draw the lines right on my workbench. This is the distance between the legs.

I now take my square and mark a line 7 1/2" down from the top on each leg. Look at the photo of the *Sofia Entry Table* and see that the lower arched stretchers are behind the front legs and in front of the back legs. This is the joint that we are marking. Make your mark on the back of the front legs and on the front of the back legs. Assemble the right side legs with the front and back stretchers and set them aside. Do the same with the left side.

Now stand them up on the lines you drew on your work table. The left and right legs need to be 36" apart. Stand the right side assembly to the right of the line on the right and the left assembly to the left for the line on the left. Check to see that the back legs are placed correctly. If your mortises at the top are a bit loose, clamp the leg section as in the photo so that the legs sit firmly and so that you can mark the structure without everything falling like a house of cards.

This next part may seem a bit challenging, but again, if you take this one step at a time, I think you'll find that it's pretty straightforward.

Pick up your front arched stretcher and make a mark, across the grain, on the front, 18" to the right of the center mark. You drew that center mark when you laid out the arches. Now draw a mark, across the grain 18" to the left of your center mark. Do the same thing with the back arched stretcher but this time mark the back side. Now you have two parallel lines, centered on your arched stretcher, that are 36" apart. This is the distance between the left and right legs.

Take two clamps (Quick Grip Clamps that you can adjust with one hand come in very handy here) and, with care, clamp your front lower arched stretcher to the back of the front legs, 7 1/2" from the top and 36" from left to right, centered. Notice in the photo below that I am working my way up to the line. Do the same thing with the back legs. Re-check everything to make sure that all your lines "line up." You can also double-check everything by making sure that the straight edges (inside of legs and top of stretchers) are square.

DELTA
FRONT LEG
BACK LEG
BL

BL
FRONT

Assuming that everything checks out, pick up your razor knife and mark where the legs and stretchers meet. The top line will be square to the inside of the leg and the bottom mark will be curved on the bottom of each leg. Make sure that it is a crisp and accurate line that you can "read." Before you disassemble the base assembly, make sure that you have everything labeled. Left front (LF), right front (RF), left back (LB), and right back (RB) can apply to legs, tenons on front to back stretchers, and on the lower arched stretchers. Now that everything is correctly labeled, take everything apart carefully.

Lay out your four legs with the side that you just marked facing up. Place the legs together so that the arched parts are outside and the flat parts are touching. Lay them exactly side by side to make sure that the top mark is even on all legs at 7 1/2".

Now look at the lower mark, which is a slightly arched. It will look almost straight but in fact it is a segment of an arch. Lay your marking knife on the part closest to the upper line (on the straight part of the leg) and make another mark across the grain. This will be parallel to the first line that you made. Make sure that you lay your square on the inside (straight) part of the leg, otherwise your mark will not be parallel.

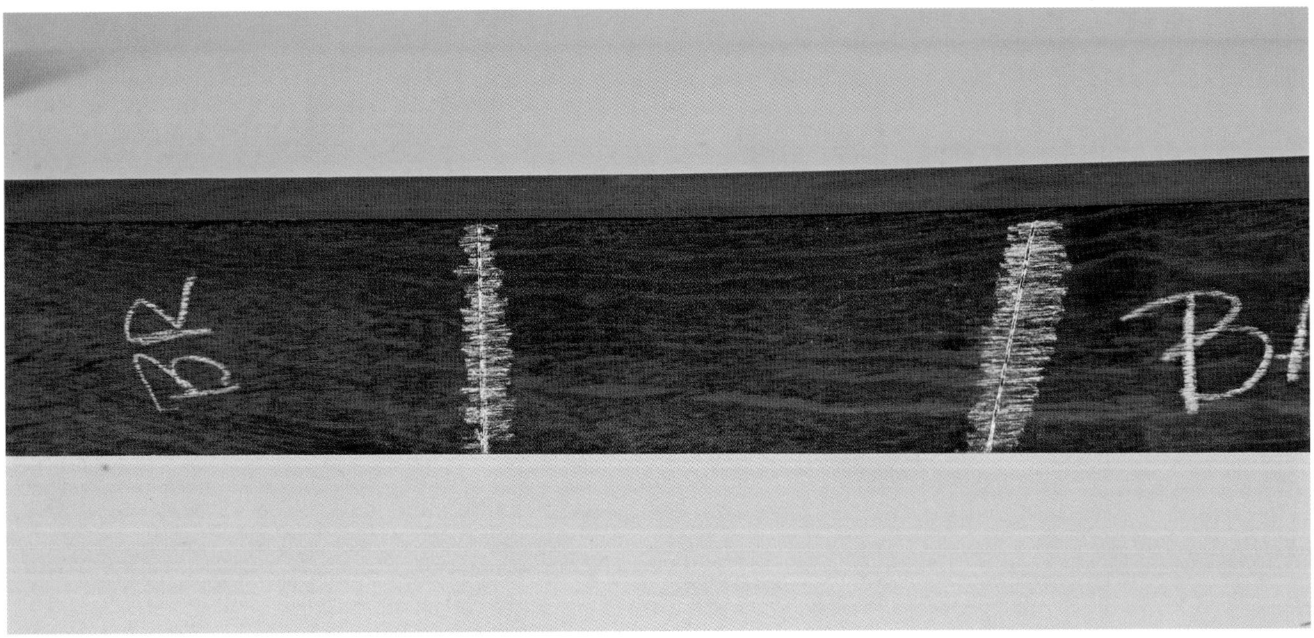

Now, make a 1/4" scribe line on the two sides of the leg where you made the two parallel marks. One 1/4" scribe line will tell you where to cut. The other one will prevent tear out. Do this to all the legs. **Do not** mark where the arch is at this point. When you have all the legs marked, take everything to the table saw.

Raise your saw blade 1/4" and carefully cut out the open half lap joint. I don't use a dado blade because of the scoring marks the outside blades make, which would be visible on the legs. If you have a combination blade, you might want to use this because the raker tooth on the blade will leave a flat bottom to your cut. When you have finished cutting the four legs, your task will be to finish cutting the bottom arch of the open mortise, which will mate with the arched stretcher.

The trick here is that we are not going to cut a segment of an arch but rather a straight line. Think of any curved brick building. Straight bricks are frequently used to form the outline of a curved façade brick building. It's the same thing here.

BR
BL

I start by scoring, with my knife, the full line that I am going to cut. I use my Japanese dovetail saw to make this cut. I also use a guide block to insure that I am cutting perpendicular to my line so that I get a clean fit with the stretcher. If I made this cut, or others by hand, day in and day out, I'm sure that I would not need a guide. But given that I don't, I prefer to be safe rather than sorry.

Make your cut 1/4" deep and then clean it up with a chisel. Take your arched piece and test to see if your cut fits. When all four legs are cut, re-assemble the base again and make sure that everything fits as it should.

We're getting there, just a few more steps. We're going to join the upper top stretcher to the left and right front to back stretcher so that it appears to pierce through them. The upper stretcher is item number 6 from the "actual bill of fare." It is 1" thick by 2" wide by 46" long.

SONGS FOR SARAH
FRONT LEG
BACK LEG

BL

Sand this piece now to 240. Because it is a double lap joint, if you cut it and then sand it, you will make your joint fit too loosely. I mark the cuts that I will make with the base assembled. You might need to use clamps to ensure that nothing moves, shifts or falls as you mark.

First mark the middle of the 15" long front to back stretcher and then make another mark 1/2" to the left and right of that first score line. Now take the 46" long stretcher and lay it on top of the score lines on the front to back stretcher. Center the 46" long piece so that an equal length is overhanging the front to back stretchers, to the left and right. Now mark the 46" long piece where it crosses the front to back stretchers. Finally mark the top stretcher "L" for left side and "R" for right side to insure that you line up the joints correctly when you re-assemble the piece.

Take the 46 inch long piece to the table saw. Find or make a test piece from scrap wood that is 2" in height, just like your top stretcher. It should be about 6 or 7 inches long. Set the blade height to 1" (half the height of the piece we're working on, which is 2"). When you establish that you have the height correct on your test piece, cut out both joints. Take the upper stretcher back to the assembled base and fit it back onto the front to back stretchers. If you have a hard time fitting the front to back stretchers into the slots that you just cut, find where they are rubbing or where they are too tight and make the cuts that need adjusting. Be careful that you don't take too much off and make the joint sloppy. When you have it "right," double-check your marks on the front to back stretchers and disassemble the base. Cut the half lap joints on the front to back stretchers. Check the cut with its mating piece for fit and depth.

F to B
OUTSIDE

LEFT SIDE

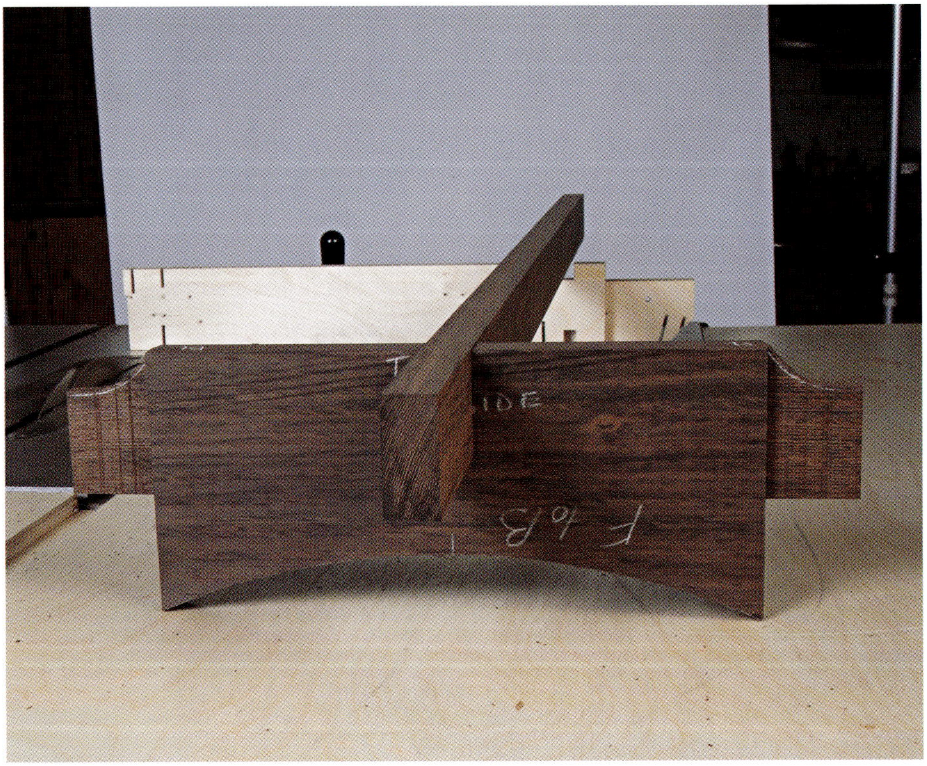
F to B

Mitering the Two Lower and One Upper Stretchers

There are certain shapes that we immediately associate with different cultures and periods of history. You can travel to Spain and immediately recognize the influence of the Moors in the mosaics of castles and fortifications. Middle East Mosques, Onion Domes in Russia, both tell us where we are without uttering a word.

I try to employ similar techniques in the *Sofia Entry Table*. The overhanging top, I hope, will recall the roof of the famous Imperial Palace and other Japanese structures, as will the beveled front arches and the curves of the legs and aprons.

This step in making the base is fairly straightforward. I mitre the ends of the stretchers at about 15°. Start by marking the cut that you will make in pencil at the end of the arched stretchers. The cut is wider at the top and angled in towards the legs on each side. Take the time to mark each cut that you will make. The danger in not marking the cut is that you might make the cut in the wrong direction, so make sure that you can visualize it clearly before you cut it.

I set up my mitre gauge to 15° and attach a backer/sacrificial fence as a quick way to line up my cut and to minimize tearout. Make a test cut with only the sacrificial backer being cut. Now, take your lower stretcher, set the flat, top side on the miter gauge and line up the edge of the stretcher with the saw kerf on the sacrificial backer. If this is unclear, see the photo. Make your cut. Flip the board, end over end and cut the other end. Voila! Do the same to the other stretcher and also to the top stretcher.

SONGS FOR SARAH
DELTA

Curving the Inside of the Legs

Disassemble the base and put the legs aside. We are going to cut out the square, inside parts of the four legs so that we have curved legs on the outside *and* the inside. You can refer to the patterns that I provided. The scale is 1 box equals 1 square inch. Make your pattern as before, cut it out, smoothly, on heavy weight paper and then draw the inside leg curve on the four legs. The segment that you are going to cut runs approximately from 8 1/2" below the top of the leg to the bottom of the leg. Go back to the band saw and make your cuts about 1/16" fat of the line.

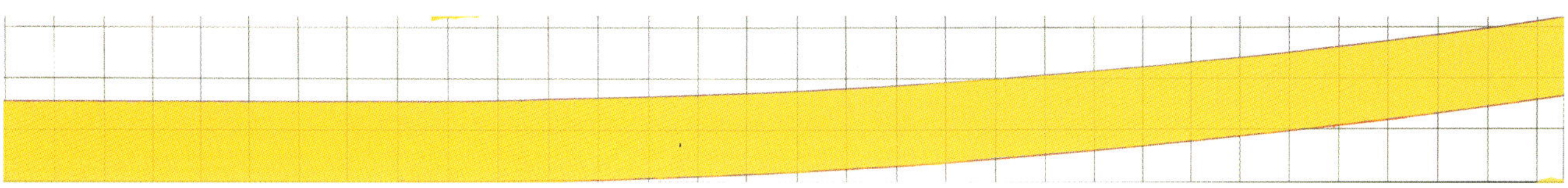

I then take the legs to my horizontal sander and carefully sand the curve back to the line that I drew on the leg. The most important part here, if you use a horizontal sander, is to make sure your table is 90° to the sanding platen.

I would suggest that you assemble everything one last time, just to make sure that everything fits correctly and looks right. Rather than assembling the base on your workbench, place it on the floor, this time, as it will be seen in real life. Now, make a note of everything that you will be sanding. All the parts need to be final sanded before the pieces are glued together. Five pieces are already sanded to their final destination. What remains to be sanded are the four legs. But in addition to these, you should also sand the end grain of the lower arched stretchers, the end grain of the upper stretcher, the end grain of the through tenon on the front to back stretcher (be careful to keep it square by using wood sanding block) and also the end grain of the top of the legs which will be visible. I usually sand the end grain to 400 so that it will take the oil finish evenly and not appear darker than any other part of the furniture.

When all the sanding is finished, you are ready to glue your parts together. (Because I used wenge, an exotic wood for the base, I wiped all the joints to be glued with lacquer thinner before I applied glue to insure that there were no oils on the wood that would weaken the glue joint.) I find it easier to glue the left side (3 pieces, front and back legs and a front to back stretcher) and right side (3 pieces) rather than gluing the front and then the back. I place a small, thin amount of glue in the open leg mortise using a small paintbrush. NOTE WELL: Neatness counts when gluing. I also place a small amount, very thinly in the center of the open mortise. I then mate the two legs to the stretcher. If I feel I want tighter contact, I will use a clamp around the tenon to make a tighter fit for gluing. Lay the left side to dry and do the same for the right side. You will notice that the cut away at the top of the open mortise and tenon is a bit proud (high) of the leg top. We actually planned for this earlier and we will clean this up after we have finished gluing. Let the left and right sections dry over night. Before I proceed with more gluing, I will clean up any squeeze out using an old chisel, knife or combination thereof. When that glue has dried, I reassemble the left side legs and the right side with the arched stretchers.

Next I take masking tape and mask the outline of the legs as that outline crosses the arched stretcher so that I know where to apply glue. Now glue the lower arched stretcher and the upper stretcher to the left and right side. You'll need six clamps. Using a small paintbrush, I start with the front arched stretcher. Coat the inside of the open half lap joint on the leg, staying about 1/4" away from the sides so that there is little or no ooze of glue. I'll place a thin dab of glue on the corresponding face of the stretcher and then mate the lower arched stretcher to the corresponding leg and clamp these in place. You will find that by picking up the opposite side (the other side that you will glue next) you can stand the base upright and easily glue the other side. Once you get both legs together, check to make sure that your legs are 36" apart at the top. Proceed to the back lower stretcher and repeat the process that you just completed. If you need to use two clamps, do so.

40 39 38 37 36 35 34 33 32 31 30

Lastly, take the top stretcher, place glue at the bottom of the lap joint and mate the pieces and clamp them together. Put them aside and let them dry overnight. When I unclamp everything the next day, I put the table on a flat surface to see if it sits flat.

I will nail 1/4" nylon glides to the legs. I do this on every piece of furniture that I make. It prevents undue wear and tear on wood that touches the floor as it is moved and cleaned. A piece will also rest more solidly if it rests at four points rather than over its entire length as in the case of a sideboard or chest of drawers.

If everything was cut squarely and carefully, it should sit flat. If it doesn't, I don't despair. Assuming that one leg will be off by less than 1/8", I make a note of which leg is too long. I flip the base over, on a rug or other clean surface and nail the glides to the 3 feet that are the same. If the leg is 1/16" or 3/32" too high, I then go to the sander and take the corresponding amount off the glide and nail it on the long leg. Stand the base back on a flat surface and, lo and behold, like magic, it's perfect.

Since I had the base turned upside down for the previous photos, I thought I'd include a photo of the repair that we made to the leg with epoxy early on in the project. It took me a while to locate where the problem was, but with difficulty, I finally found it.

The last step in completing the base is to clean up the transition of the tenon cut away on each leg. The cut away part of the tenon should be about 1/16" proud of the top of the leg. The end grain top of the leg should already be sanded so, in order to not scratch it, I mask off the area. I use a Dremel Tool; you can use a fine rasp or a piece of sand paper taped around a thick dowel. Work you way down carefully. Work on the back legs first. Finally, slightly bevel the four edges of the through tenon.

Congratulations, you have finished making the base.

Making the Shelf

The key to laying out the shelf is to be flexible and to check your numbers as you lay out the individual pieces. The legs are supposed to be 36" apart but things happen, and next thing you know, the front legs are at 36 1/8" and the back legs are at 35 15/16". Don't despair. The gaps between the 14 pieces that make up the shelf are the "back door" that we will use to make this work while making it appear as if you laid it out perfectly. The key is to make adjustments as you go and spread out whatever "problems" you have over the 13 spaces between the 14 slats. By and large, your eye will not pick up a change of 1/64" or less.

In designing *The Sofia Line*, I have always enjoyed using contrasting species of wood: walnut and cherry, curly maple and cherry, curly birch and mahogany, and lately bubinga and wenge. In general, I use one species on the vertical members and a different one on the horizontal surfaces. In the *Sofia Entry Table*, the base that we have just finished making contains all of the vertical pieces, i.e., legs, and five stretchers. The shelf and the plank top are our horizontal pieces, and, as such, they will be made of bubinga, wild figured and curly for the top, straight grained for the shelf. This difference in texture and figure will be another counterpoint between the shelves and the top.

Over the years I have had several designers and woodworkers suggest that the design would be "better" if I made the shelf out of a solid plank like the table top. My instinct tells me that this one change would "kill" the design. I think the table "works" because it is able to convey lightness or space, if you will, even though the piece is 58" wide and 17" deep. The convex curve of the front of the slatted shelf contrasts with the concave arch of the stretcher below. This in turn will contrast with the more natural edge or in this case, the straight edge of the plank top that will crown the piece. Additionally one of the great loves of my life has been music. I am reminded of a marimba and the piano when I see the table. I like to think of the pieces in the *Sofia Line* as music in 3D.

There is one more element that the shelf with slats introduces and that is the use of hardware, i.e. the black screw that secures the individual slats to the arched stretcher. I think of this element as a link to the wrought iron hardware seen on traditional Japanese furniture. It is a small decorative detail and a secondary reinforcement to the front and back legs that adds strength and stability to the piece. I also like the contrast of wood (smooth and shiny) and metal (rough and dull.) I use trim head black, square drive #7 screws that are 1" long purchased from McFeeley's Square Drive Inc. (www.mcfeeleys.com). I would not use slotted or Phillips head screws, they "read" like drywall screws.

I begin by looking at the board that will yield the wood for the 14 slats, which need to finish at 17" long by 2 7/16" by 3/8" thick. Since bubinga is fairly expensive, I am going to resaw my pieces. I will need 7 boards 17" long by 2 3/4" wide by 1" thick. I will add an 8th board for test pieces and in case I have an unforeseen problem with one of the slats. The board that I am using is almost 6" wide and almost 1 1/8" thick. I got lucky; it was considered 4/4. I will joint and plane the board lightly to a fat 1". Next I cross cut my lengths to 17" on my cross cut sled at the table saw. After that, I rip each board to 2 3/4". At the band saw I resaw the 7 boards plus the extra one to just under 1/2". Next I will re-rip each of the slats to 2 7/16". Finally, I will lightly plane the 16 slats to just 3/8" thickness. Before moving on to lay out the shelf, I will sand all the pieces, top and bottom, to 220 grit (50 microns.)

Laying Out the Slats

Take slats 1 through 7 and push them up against the left leg. Take slats 8 through 14 and push them up against the right leg. Measure the distance between slats 7 and 8 in the front, above the front stretcher and in the rear above the rear stretcher. If they are not the same, take the smaller number and divide by 13 (the number of spaces between the slats) to begin calculating the thickness that your spacer needs to be. When I pushed 1 through 7 to the left and 8 to 14 right, the measurement was 1 13/16". Convert your fractions to decimals so that the result is easier to divide. If you need help with this, as I always do, you can Google "decimal to inch converter" and consult a chart. 1 13/16" converts to 1.8123. So 1.8125 divided by 13 is 0.139. This number is a hair less than 1/8" plus a 1/64". I will make my spacer at 1/8". You can make your spacer with a planer or on the table saw, whichever you are most comfortable using. If your numbers are different, just go through the same process to determine the thickness of your spacer.

Marking and Cutting the Counter Sink for the Screws

Now take a look at your 14 pieces as they sit next to one another and paying attention to the grain, lay them out as you would like to see them. Here's a chance to use your artist's eye to play with pattern or to break it up. You decide.

Once you've done that, take a board or piece of plywood, clamp it at the shelf height to the back of the rear legs so that you have a straight line to butt your 14 pieces against.

Take a piece of masking tape and number all your slats. I always number left to right. I write the numbers with myself standing in front of the piece looking at it. I want to be sure that I do not accidentally flip a board around.

Now move all the slats except numbers 1 and 14 to the center. Leave 1 and 14 touching the leg. Mark on these two slats where the center of the stretcher, below the slat, is located. Mark both the front and the rear of number 1 and 14.

Now place slats 2 through 7 to the left, as before, and 8 through 13 to the right. Make sure that all slats are up against the board clamped to the back legs. Take a straight edge or yard stick and draw a straight line across the slats, connecting the marks made on numbers 1 and 14.

I have measured again and you can see that the distance for my 13 gaps is 1 13/16".

Take each slat and mark the center point of each line at 1 7/32". Set up your drill press to drill a 1/4" diameter hole 1/8" deep. You can also set up your drill press fence so that the center point is at 1 7/32" from the fence. I will also use my test piece to be sure that my depth is correct. Place the head of the actual screw that you will use into the hole. You want the screw head to sit below the height of the shelf. 1/8" will do it. Try it on a test piece first; when you have it correct, you are ready to move to the 14 slats. Take your 14 pieces, line up the pencil line that you drew on each piece over the centerline of the arched stretcher and drill your holes. There will be one hole in the front and one in the back of each slat. Watch for tear out, make each cut purposefully. Clean up wood chips as you go along so that each hole is centered. If you get a chip stuck between your board and the fence, your hole will be off center and noticeable.

Setting the Individual Pieces

Mark the middle point of the front and back stretchers between the legs. This should be about 18" from each leg. This will be your primary reference point. Ideally the gap between slat numbers 7 and 8 will be centered on this line. Work in towards the middle from both ends. I like to start on my left.

I start the next step by marking the depth that I will pre drill the hole for the screw with a piece of masking tape. Take stretcher #1 and lay it against the back fence and against the left leg. Clamp both the front and back to the stretcher, but leaving enough space to get your hand held drill bit (1/8") into the predrilled counter sink that we made in each of the boards. Drill down no more than an inch so that you don't drill through the arched stretcher. I use a #7 1" square drive trim screw. Screw the front and back of the slat in place. Don't over tighten, and make sure the screw head is below the surface of the wood. Move to the other side of the base and do the same with slat #14.

Place your spacer between one and two and screw in number 2. Go to the other side and do the same with number 13.

At this point I place all the remaining slats on the stretcher, remove the spacers, and push them all to one side and measure how much space I have left on the front and the back. Divide by 11. Use the decimal to inch converter if you need to. Make your adjustment with the gap. Do not cut the spacer down. If you need to make the spacer slightly thinner or fatter, make a new one, no more than 1/64" different than your original spacer. Your goal is to come back to the original spacer. Continue in this fashion until all the slats are in place.

When you get to the last two slats, try to divide the last three remaining gaps evenly. I place the back of 7 and 8 in first and then the front.

I like to have the back of the slats meet the back legs at the mid-point 3/4". Right now they are even with the back leg. I mark slat 1 and 14, 3/4" in from the back, take my straight edge and mark that point with my razor knife or fine point pencil. We will make this cut when we cut the front of the slats.

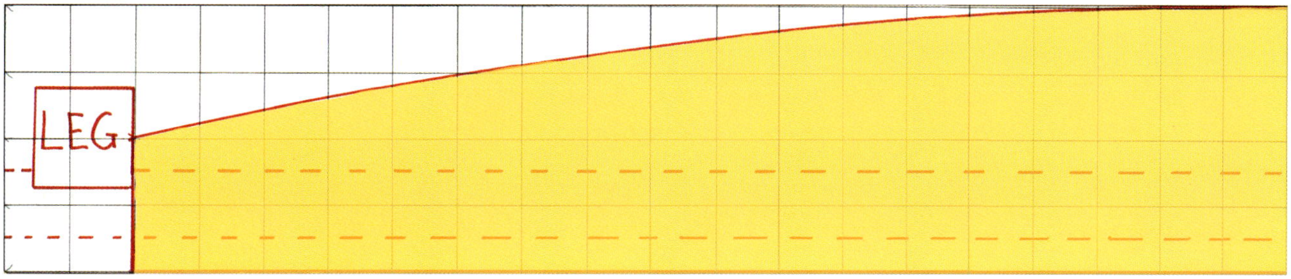

I have provided you with a half pattern of the front curve for the slats. (NOTE WELL: I have drawn in the leg as a point of reference to help you visualize how to lay the sketch before tracing the line onto the slats. As before, the scale is 1 box equals 1 square inch.)

I trace the curve onto the 14 slats. When you remove your pattern, take a moment and be sure that you have clearly marked the arch segment on all 14 pieces. Unscrew and remove each slat carefully. It is imperative that you number all of the slats on the bottom side now, as you remove them from the base. At the tablesaw I cut the back of the slat square on the knife mark that I made earlier.

At the band saw I cut the arc segment on each slat slightly proud of my line. I then take each piece to my horizontal sander and refine it, trying to leave the slightest hint of my pencil line.

I screw slat number 2 through 13 back onto the stretchers. Hint: *use new screws to ensure that your bit does not slip out and damage the wood.* Place numbers 1 and 14 in their space but only screw them in loosely. Take a good look at the arch on the slats and see if any adjustments have to be made. I do this with my random orbital sander on 2 through 13. I do it free handed using 220 sandpaper on the disc so as not to be overly aggressive. Don't use the random orbital sander on 1 or 14, as you will surely damage the leg with the sander. If the two end pieces need a final adjustment, take them off and make your adjustment with a sanding block. Once you have adjusted the front, double check the back and make any necessary refinements there, screw in the last two pieces.

Making the Top

Besides using the *Sofia Entry Table* as I had envisioned when I first designed it, my clients' vision is often more expansive than my own. I have been asked to adapt the design for servers in the dining room and behind sofas, expanded it to be used in public places of worship and small private retreats. Some have requested that the top be made of stone and others of glass. I sometimes feel like a parent who raises a child and delights at seeing their offspring strike out on new and different paths that they, the parent, had never envisioned. I take great pride and comfort in knowing that the design is what I call "approachable." People seem willing to adapt what I make to their own uses. But in the end, for me, the most satisfying part of making this table is finding just the right plank or small slab of wood to place on top of the base.

In this last section, I'm going to talk more about my *process* than about the jointing and planing of the plank top. Some of you might have heavy-duty machinery and can do it as I do. Others will be comfortable getting out their hand planes and scrapers. Still others may get out the electric planes or even belt sanders. There is no *one* way to do this "right." I believe that there is a woodworking equivalent to what Duke Ellington once said about music, "if it sounds good it *is* good."

There are some simple guidelines that I always follow when working solid wood that are especially true when working with wide boards. Know your logger. I have confidence with the two that I use. I know that the wood was properly cut, aged, cured, dried, and stacked before I purchase it. I also try, as much as possible, to work with boards that have stayed flat.

Once I begin working on a plank, I make sure that it always has air circulating around the top and bottom. When you are finished working with the plank, or even if you stop to take a short break, place it on sticks so that air gets to the bottom side also. Do not lay the plank on a table with the other side open to the air. If you lay it down that way, no matter how flat the board is, it will warp, twist or cup. Even for a short period of time, if the plank gets air on one side and none on the other it will lose or take on moisture that will cause an imbalance in the plank's equilibrium and problems may ensue.

Another important rule of thumb for me is to "work conservatively." I take off a little at a time every day, if possible no more than 1/4". It's okay with me if the wood moves because I know that tomorrow I can come back and have another chance at straightening it.

I always make the top to this piece of furniture out of a single plank or small slab. I think that a set of matching boards would also work with this design. Perhaps one of the matching boards might have a natural edge or perhaps neither would. Once again, take some time and look at what you have with your artist's eye. You decide. Unless there are special needs dictated by the space where the table will "live," I prefer a top that is 16 to 18 inches wide. I have made the entry tabletop as narrow as 12" wide with the base being only 10" wide. That particular table resides in a very narrow hallway.

The first rule of thumb in choosing a board for the top, when you make this table, is to start out with a board that is flat and that has no twists. The base does not have a great deal of mass, so unlike a desk or a dining table, with aprons that extend close to the edge of the top, you will not be able to make the top of the entry table lay flat when you attach it to the base. I stay away from planks that have serious defects or splits. Those types of planks call a lot of attention to themselves in a manner that I don't think complements this design. I usually start with a plank that is 5/4 (1 1/4") thick. In the case of the curly bubinga, it was 6/4 (1 1/2"). I will make the top approximately 1 1/8" thick.

I start by taking my plank to the radial arm saw and cutting an inch or two off the end of the board to ensure that there are no cracks or splits on the piece that will become the top. Once you make the cut, look first at the piece that you have cut off. Is there a crack? Just to be sure, I sometimes take that cut off piece and hit it on the ground or the edge of the radial arm saw table. If it breaks easily, there may have been a crack that was too small to see. I'll cut another inch or so off the end of the board until I'm satisfied that there are no cracks remaining that might come back to "bite me" after I've finished making the table.

The finished plank will be 58" long so I will cross cut my rough length to about 62" or 64". Next, I will lay the plank on a pair of sawhorses and look at it from every side and angle. I do this to see if perhaps I missed something in my initial "look." Is there some interesting grain that I missed? Does the side that I thought was going to be the bottom, now seem like it should be the top? Does the edge that I was going to cut off now seem to be more interesting if the bevel of the edge is up rather than down? Sometimes, I'll place the raw top on the base to get a better perspective. If I'm not convinced one way or another, I'll leave the top on the base and go work on something else or pay bills in the office. When I emerge a little while later, I'll glance over at the piece. Now, I'm seeing it from a different angle, in different light. This "walking around" time is invaluable in making the aesthetic decisions that affect the final outcome of making any piece of furniture. (Hint: *If you really want to see the piece from different angles, sweep the floor around where you are working and while you are doing that, glance over at the piece while you sweep. You will not only help yourself to understand the piece better, you will have a cleaner and nicer environment to work in and once again you are reinforcing the idea of being "purposeful" in everything that you are doing in your arena.*)

Once I have decided how the top will sit on the base, I give myself visual notes with chalk on the top of the plank. I will draw a straight line on the back that is relatively parallel to the front. I also draw lines across the grain to mark where the two ends will be cut. If I want to move the lines an inch or so, I just take a damp rag and remove the chalk lines and start again.

Next I joint and plane the plank over the course of two days. Since this piece will have a rectangular top, I ripped the front on the table saw parallel to the back. After that I sand the plank to my final thickness at 1 1/8". Remember that if there is a cabinet shop in your area with a wide belt sander, you could do the same thing.

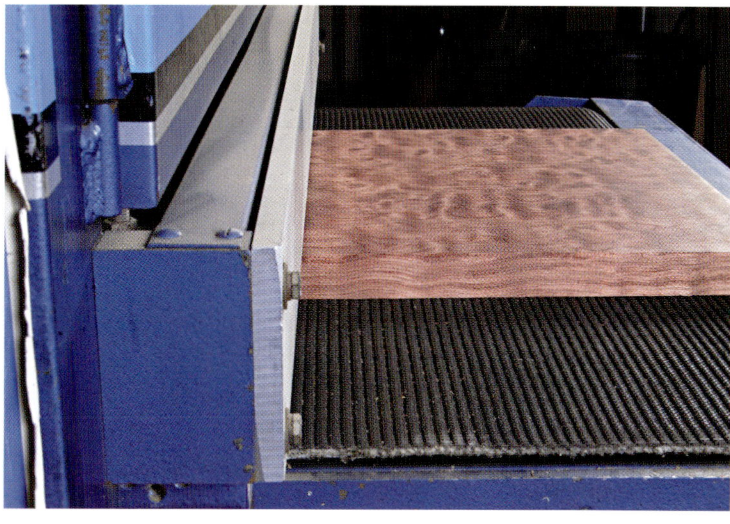

I go back to the table saw to cross cut the top to length. I use a backer board and my razor knife to eliminate tear out. When I have finished milling the top to its final dimension, I will lay the board on my work bench and write myself some notes to insure that I don't lose track of what is front, back or which edges will be beveled etc. Once that is clear I usually place the top onto the base just to see if I like how it looks. If you are not sure, walk away, go get a cup of coffee or call it a day. If you come back relaxed and rested you may see the piece with different "eyes."

The last step in making this top is to cut a 60° bevel edge on the underside of the sides and front. This profile can be cut with a router or on the shaper.

If I am making a top that will incorporate a natural edge, I will look at the front edge and, using a wire brush, I will clean any debris or dirt from the natural edge. If there is bark left on the edge I will carefully get rid of it because the bark will eventually fall off. I am careful not to gouge the natural edge while removing the bark. I have a set of dental picks to help with this task as well as rasps, files, and other implements of digging and "destruction" that I have acquired over the years. Sometimes I'll use a Dremel Tool. It all depends. Like anything else in life, if you want to do it well, you'll need to practice and you'll need to get comfortable doing this. If you are hesitant to try it on your top, practice on the edge that you are going to cut off or on the edge of the piece that is left over. You can even take a plank of wood that has no "natural" edge and play "mother nature" and try to put a natural edge on it and see if you can make it look natural. (Hint: *follow the grain line along the length of the board with a saber saw angled downward about 15°. If I learned how to do this, you can too!*)

Now that the top is prepared as I had planned, I will place it back on the base, centering it left to right and "play" with the front and back overhangs. I usually try to have a half-inch overhang in the back and 1 1/2" in front. However, this is where the question of how the table will be viewed comes into play. If the table is viewed from afar, you will see a lot of the base. But if it's in a hallway and you don't get far away from it, you may not see much of the base unless you have less of an overhang. Again, your artist's eye comes into play.

Another element that can be "shown off" is where the table top appears to float above the legs. If you have a front edge that wanders, you could reveal more of the top of one leg than the other. Now you can see a detail of joinery that is not evident from afar and so you have given the viewer an unexpected surprise. This is the fun part that you get to experiment with and control. If you have not guessed it by now I will admit to you that, for me, the joy of creativity in making furniture is in the process of bringing a design to life; in making those choices that will make every piece unique and a world unto itself. I believe that good design allows for such opportunities and discoveries not just for the maker but also for the user and the viewer.

The very last detail is securing the top to the base. We will use the table clip that we spoke about earlier. The lower part of the clip will fit into the kerf that we cut into the inside of the front to back stretchers. The upper part will be screwed into the underside of the plank top. The clip, trapped in the groove, pulls the table down to the stretcher and still allow the table to expand and contract with the change of seasons, temperature, and humidity. I make a mark where the screw hole is with an awl, remove the top and pre-drill a pilot hole for the screw, and then, using a black screw (also available from McFeeley's), I will screw it in by hand.

Most woodworkers that I have ever met have their own "bible" on wood preparation. Some who are "true believers" believe that anyone who does not follow this "true" path produces inferior work. I'm in the "if it looks good, functions correctly, and feels good to the touch, it is good" camp. I've seen everything – from planed to scraped to sanded and rustic to "I just like to leave it raw!" pieces of furniture. Those that were done purposefully and with thought I enjoyed seeing and touching. I'm guessing that their makers and those persons for whom the pieces were made still feel the same way about the furniture. Choose you own path. Plane, scrape or sand or combinations thereof and be true to it, study it, know what works best and what doesn't. But whatever way you choose, do it well, carefully, and most importantly, purposefully.

I sand. Even if I plane some parts of the project, I will finish by sanding. In the shop we use only 3M Mylar backed micron sandpaper, which I purchase from the Japan Woodworker in California (www.japanwoodworker.com). I use 8 hole hook and loop. After all parts are sanded on the wide belt sander to 120 grit, we start at 120 microns (120 grit equivalent) and work our way through 80 microns (180 grit), 50 microns (240 grit) and end at 30 microns (400 grit). One main difference with micron paper is that unlike standard grits which have a greater percentage of different grits mixed in (120 grit for example will also have coarser grits) micron is much more uniform so the scratch pattern is more consistent and by the time you arrive at 400 it is virtually invisible to the naked eye.

This sandpaper is more expensive than most but my experience from having used it for more than twelve years is that it lasts longer and you can work faster than with other papers. On end grain we also sand to 30 microns and there is no darkening of the end grain when a finish is applied. I am frequently surprised when reading woodworking articles on the finishing of cherry. Authors will mention how cherry is prone to get blotchy. I always find myself commenting to the magazine, "you're either working with poor quality cherry or you have not prepared your material sufficiently well. What they are calling blotch is really figure that has not been prepared (sanded or planed) properly." Since it is not yet prepared properly, light can't enter into the fibers and is trapped there unable to reflect back so it looks "blotchy."

Having been purposeful to this point on making the piece, my hope is that you will be purposeful in this most important step of sanding. You are at the start of the final lap. Now is not the time to let up. Sand carefully. Get out the spotlights and shine them on your surfaces as you are preparing the top for finish. It will pay you handsomely in elevating your work to a higher level of achievement.

Final Sanding and Finishing

At this point in the process, the base is complete and the top is made. I'm ready for final sanding and finishing. The first thing I do is clean up a bit. I put away tools and get rid of scraps of wood I can't reuse. I'm doing this so that I can clear up horizontal surfaces. This will let me lay out all the parts that I need to finish. It will also help ensure that I don't damage or ding parts as I'm moving them around.

I'm also looking at the table out of the corner of my eye while I'm doing all this. I'm seeing my work from different angles as it will be seen in real life. Don't be surprised if you find yourself saying, "Next time I would make this curve slightly different." It is all part of the maturation process that you will experience.

Next, I will carefully unscrew the 14 pieces that make up the shelf and lay them on stickers so that they won't cup or warp. The same goes for the tabletop. (Hint: *I try to use stickers that are half rounds so that there is as little wood contact as possible.*)

Once I have everything sanded, I am ready to proceed to finishing. Having all the pieces laid out will guarantee that parts will dry properly. I tend to use three different finishes or combinations thereof on my furniture. They are as follows:

1. Formby's High Gloss Tung Oil. I use this with cherry especially. I think it works best with casework, bases, and legs, but I do not use it on tabletops. Use the High Gloss. In three coats, it won't get glossy and it has fewer chemicals and additives than the satin finish.

2. Tried and True Linseed Oil Varnish. This is my preferred finish for tabletops. It is unlike any oil that you have ever used but takes getting used to in application. I find it to be labor intensive so I tend to use it only for tabletops. It is an excellent finish for walnut.

3. J.S. Moser's Danish Oil. This is a good finish for tabletops and also for casework.

For casework, bases, etc., I use 3 coats of Formby's or Moser's finishes. For tops I usually use 5 or 6 coats. If you are going to use these finishes and are unfamiliar with them I strongly suggest that you prepare a test piece prepped just like the table that you have made. Follow the instructions on the can and then finish the piece just like you are going to finish your entry table.

For a more detailed discussion of how I finish my furniture, you can go to my web page www.ortizstudios.com and link to ortizstudios blog and follow that to the section on "finishing."

Some Final Thoughts

In my more philosophical moments I sense that, for me, woodworking is more a calling, a vocation if you will, than a career. Ultimately, I think that woodworking is about legacy, what I will leave behind long after I am gone. With a little luck and someone else's care, I hope that the furniture that I make will be my emissary to the 22nd century. It can be the same for you.

I have used the word "purposeful" many times in this book, when referring to how I think you should approach making furniture. The truth is that it can be applied to every aspect of our lives: work, play, family, careers, etc. You name it – it applies. That is the reason that I believe that there are no trade secrets, just purposeful hard work and attention to detail. I'm willing to bet that this is what Emeril, Michael, and Tiger, to name a few, have found...that everything matters and that everything we do and think is connected to the results we achieve. That is what I have found. There are no secrets, just purposeful living and hard work. Whether it's cooking, basketball, golf, furniture making, plumbing, gardening, etc., you can achieve and produce wonderful things. My hope is that perhaps something that you have read or learned in this book will be of use to you in achieving whatever you pursue.